DESIGNING MY FUTURE

DESIGNING MY FUTURE

Rishit Kalra

GenNext Publication

First Published, 2018

Published by

GenNext Publication
5, Ansari Road
Daryaganj, New Delhi-110002
Phone: 9811692060
E-mail: gennextpublication@hotmail.com

Printed at: G. Print Process, Delhi.

Cataloging in Publication Data—DK

Courtesy: D.K. Agencies (P) Ltd. <docinfo@dkagencies.com>

Kalra, Rishit, author.

Designing my future / by Rishit Kalra.
pages cm
ISBN 9789380223278

1. Conduct of life. 2. Self-actualization (Psychology)
I. Title.

LCC BF637.S4K35 2018 | DDC 158.1 23

Let us take out time to enjoy simple things in life

Contents

Why I wrote this book?

In my book, I have tried to pen down all those lessons that I have learnt till now. At this age I don't actually know how successful would I be as an adult but yes I have complete confidence in myself and in my ideas. It would be a great honour and success for me if my young readers get inspired by these lessons and it could be helpful to them in designing their future. My best wishes to all my readers.

Acknowledgement

I would like to express my gratitude to all those who saw me through this book, to all those who provided support, talked things over, read, wrote, offered comments, allowed me to quote their remarks and assisted me in editing, proof reading and designing.

I would like to thank the team of GenNext Publication for enabling me to publish this book. I would also like to thank my School Principal Ma'am Mrs Nita Arora and Head Mistress Ma'am Mrs R. Banopreeya who have always been my role model and source of inspiration. Above all, I would like to thank my Mother, Rinku Kalra and Father, Bhawnesh Kalra for always encouraging and showing faith in me inspite of all the thicks and thins. Last but not least I would thank my elder brother Ramit Kalra who helped me in the process of selection and edition.

Also, big thanks to all the teachers of Sri Venkateshwar International School, Dwarka. My lesson in Designing my Future is what I have learnt from them throughout these years.

Rishit Kalra

Introduction

Rishit Kalra, author of this book has written it for you to read, enjoy and apply to help you accomplish you may have desired in life. You, the reader, can read, study and apply the messages to the principles that most appeal to you. All the principles are necessary if you desire to reach your maximum potential that you received at birth. Once you have completed the book, go back and read it again and take the suggestion and repeat them until they become a part of your being. The end result of your being, study and application will help you reach your desires. But, most importantly, the ultimate result will be not what you receive in the process but the person that you become while on your journey to success.

Short Poem on Success

The road to success is always under construction. The power of positive thinking is a tool to remove all obstructions. You always get more than you give when you give more than you get. Life is not a hurdle unless you decide, not to stop till you reach success. Embrace your problems as the ingredient for growth. Feed your mind with the message of love and hope. There is always a blessing on the way, for it is the season of growth, strength and chain.

Lesson - 1

Simplicity

As I began to love myself I quit stealing my own time, and I stopped designing huge projects for the future. Today I only do what brings me joy and happiness, things I love to do and that make my hear cheer, and I do then in my way and in my own rhythm. Today I call

"SIMPLICITY"

Charlie Chaplin

Our life is like a garden. Seeds that are planted in our mental garden ultimately grow into crop that influence our success potential. Like any gardner, we must eliminate the weeds before hand and try to conserve the simplicity of our garden. Simplicity brings a sense of calm and restfulness in our lives. It is rightly advised by the elders to believe in simple living and high thinking.

Let us believe in Ourselves and perform beyond our own expectations.

Lesson - 2

Self Confidence

> The history of the world is full of men who rose to leadership, by sheer force of self-confidence, bravery and tenacity.
>
> **Mahatma Gandhi**

Each of us Create personal outcomes about ourselves that we manifest in our lives. So, a meaningful message for those of us seeking success is to model the outcome that we desire to create. There is a common heard adage that states: what goes around comes around. One cannot promise to be successful but it becomes possible only when we are in a state of mind in which we are self confident to achieve and fully determined not to quit until we got it.

> Let us all train our mind to see the good in every situation that we face day to day.

Lesson - 3

Positive Thinking

"We can complain because rose bushes have thorns or rejoice because thorn bushes have roses."

Abraham Lincoln

The first thing in the morning that I recall is that will face whatever comes today with a positive attitude. You are the master of your own thought. Your mind will only obey you. No one is good or bad. Only thinking makes it so. If we focus on what is good, we programme our subconscious minds for the goodness that will ultimately follow. If we continue to feed our mind garbage in form of negative thoughts, the results expected will not be the success that we are trying to achieve.

If we can solve a problem then there is no need to worry, And if we are unable to solve it, worry is of no use.

Lesson - 4

Say no to Worries

> Don't Worry when you are not Recognized,
>
> But strive to be worthy of Recognition.
>
> **Abraham Lincoln**

Ninety-nine per cent of things that we worry about might not happen. Worrying is waste of time. Good and bad things both will happen in life. One has to keep going without stressing over the situation that are out of our control. If life give us a lemon, in spite of complaining lets convert it into lemonade and sell to those who are thirsty. We might have a fresh start any moment we choose. One should look for the seeds that they need to cultivate and nurture into benefit that the Universe promise to bestow upon us.

> You are where you are because of the way you think and what you think.

Lesson - 5

Think Big

Think fast, think ahead, Ideas are no one's monopoly.

Dhirubhai Ambani

Always believe in yourself and think big. You are what you think. So always think big, do big, believe big, act big, work big and live big. Think big goals and win big success. Don't worry about the conditions and circumstances. Be ready for the beginning. You don't have to wait for the perfect condition. Think high and start from what you are, with what you have and where you are.

Of all the 'attitudes' we acquire, surely the attitude of gratitude is the most important and more helpful in designing my future.

Lesson - 6

Attitude of Gratitude

> Develop an attitude of gratitude and give thanks for everything that happens to you.
>
> **Brain Tracy**

An attitude of gratitude will always carry a person farther than complaining will. Compliments create thankfulness while complaints create unrest. People who complain are difficult to dealt with where as people who compliments are sought after and as fun to be around. Positive reinforcements is good for the soul and good for our neighbours. Let us work at being a good-finder rather than a faulty finder. Every step forward is a step towards achieving something bigger and better than the dissent situation.

> Don't Naiver.
>
> Make a decision.
>
> Do it now.

Lesson -7

Do it Now

> How wonderful it is that nobody need to wait a single moment before starting to improve the world.

To do a work with power, we must place our personal power in the self-confidence we already possess and use it wisely. Let's begin now by building our self confidence level. Let us repeat our positive affirmations until the affirmations become our second nature. Once these affirmations become habitual and strongly rooted in our subconscious minds, we can call on them to strengthen us and protect us against anything that may sap our self confidence. One is not sure about how much time is left. So lets do it now.

> You have the power to create anything you can imagine! Act on the ideas produced by your Imagination you will achieve sucess.

Lesson - 8

Create by Your Imagination

Imagination is the only weapons in the war against reality.

Lewis Carroll

In Orator to create your own success one must be action oriented. Without action, nothing moves. In our lives we have open spaces waiting to be filled. Avail the opportunities that are available to us but we have not taken or decided not to act on.

Voids exist in our lives-if we allow then to exist in mental, physical, social, spiritual and emotional forms, Fill the vacuum before it gets bigger and uglier and soon because a mess up for us to clean up. The best way to predict our future is to create it through our own imagination and resources.

Close the door of fear behind you and the door to success will definitely open in front of you.

Lesson - 9

No fear

> We must travel in the direction of fear.
>
> **John Berryman**

I can accept failures, everyone does at some point of life or other but I cannot stop trying at the fear of failure. Years may wrinkle our body but the fear actually wrinkles our soul. Let us take risks, be bold and let our inner self convert our fear into power and brilliance. Make of our dream are killed by fear than failure. One of the greatest fear that people live in is what others would think about our actions. Let us break this prison and try to be what we want to. With every new day hope so lets embrace it and keep moving in our journey towards success.

> Don't die before us death, Celebrate each and every breath. Be grateful to be alive and live every moment.

Lesson - 10

Live Every Moment

> My best friend is the one who brings out the best in me.
>
> **Henry Ford**

Help yourself. Love yourself. Help others in need. Accept yourself the way you are. Be like a sponge that can absorb all negativity and become that person who can emit positive vibes Life will be hard. There will be trails but that will only make you stronger. Real happiness does not only lie in money, fame, success. Real happiness be in gratitude. So be grateful to be alive. Live every moment. Work your hardest, think your smartest and dream you biggest. There will always be a reason to celebrate life. A successful person is only who is always happy.

> Live every moments, Love everyday, Because before you know it, precious time slips away.

Lesson - 11

Make More Friends

> Each friend represents
>
> A world in us, a world possibly not born until they arrive, and it is only by the meeting that a new world is born.

In order to adapt ourselves to life's many changes we must first learn to get along with others. Things can't always go our way. Individuals believe that they are holding on to their identity when they refuse to compromise, however, in most of these daily. Circumstances they are the real losers. Negotiation takes patience and expertise. When done correctly our long term success depends on it as much as we depend upon water to drink and air to breathe. Team work is the step on ladder to success. In pursuing success, always remember that real ingredient of success is to get along with and be liked by other.

> Aspire to be a giver. A giver of love,
> A giver of good vibes and A giver of strength.

Lesson - 12

Be a Giver

> The person who gives with a smile is the best giver because God loves a cheerful giver.
>
> **Mother Teresa**

The Universe rewards a giver. When you give without the expectation of return, you create a cycle that revolves around back to you. Ultimately, you are the recipient of the good you put out there. Start a ripple of going right now, and watch out for the wave of goodness that is created. Remember "what goes around comes around". If you are taken of happiness you get misery. If you are a giver of happiness you get love and joy.

The beauty of life doesn't depend on how happy you are, but how happy others can be because of you.

> We don't laugh because we're happy. We are happy because we laugh.
>
> **William James**

Lesson - 13

Laughter

Cheerfulness and contentment are great beautifiers and are famous preservers of good looks.

Charles Dickens

Laughter may truly be the best medicine. Laughter can be our personal armor against negativity and the harshners the World brings to bear on us. One should start each morning with a hearty protion of laughter wholesome laughter, like good food for our body, nourishers ourself in many ways. Thinking good thoughts create good endorphins in our physical body, and cause us to reap rewards of healthier and happier life. Always find a reason to laugh. It will add life to your life. It is a famous saying "there is very little success where there is little laughter."

Education is the most powerful weapon we can use to conquer success.

Lesson - 14

Education

Education is the best friend. An educated person is respected every where. Education beats the beauty and the youth.

Chanakya

An educated person is one who has learned how to get what he want without violating the right of others. Education is something worth cultivating. It gives us higher understanding of people, their customs, activities and beliefs. Understanding is one step closer to living in harmony rather than discord. Education is the lightening of fire in our lives which show us the way to success. The beautiful thing about learning and education is that no one take it away from us.

Better to remains silent and be thought a fool than, to speak out and remove all doubt.

Lesson - 15

Think before you Speak

Man's word is his wand filled with magic and power!

Every word you speak advertise your wisdom or ignorance. Remember this before speaking. Communication is the basic for getting along with others. Always be careful with your words. Once they are said, they can only be forgiven not forgotten. Our words will plant the seeds of either success or failure in the mind of others. Speaking right is the main ingredients for achieving a successful life. There is power in the spoken words. Avoid all inclusive restricted words such as never, nothing, every, everyone, no one and can't. They should be eliminated unless you are certain that they are correct.

If you don't design your own plan, chances are you will fall into someone else plan which are not actually planned for you.

Lesson - 16

Make Plans

> You are the master of your life. Whatever you do, you will have to bear the consequences.

Being consistently successful is a complex procedure, yet very simple, All that matter is how you go about it. Many people often shuffle between the ups and downs of life. With all the materialism processed, one thing remain a true fact-success is a mind game. It is reciprocated to those who are planned, optimistic and humble in each of the aspects. Always be a planner of your own life. You might fail at times but never give up and never stop making plans. One day you will be known for the best plans you made in life.

> Let's do something
>
> Today
>
> That Our Future Self will
>
> Thank us For.

Lesson - 17

Create opportunities

> To hell with circumstances; I create opportunities
>
> **Bruce Lee**

Don't sit around and wait for opportunity. Create it. You may sit around your whole life waiting, it's not going to just fall in your lap. You may have to make sacrifices, but who doesn't. People do it every day of their lives. Although success is a slow process but quitting won't speed it up. Know your worth. Stay true to your vision. Every day brings with it a bundle possibilities before they sink. Acknowledge the good that you already have in your life and lay it as a foundation for all abundance that you want to get.

> Fuel yourself with faith and discipline and you will be unstoppable.

Lesson - 18

Faith and Self-Discipline

> Faith is a state of mind that can be conditioned through self-discipline. Faith will accomplish.
>
> **Bruce Lee**

Fuel yourself with faith and discipline and you will be unstoppable. With faith, discipline and selfless devotion of duties, there is nothing worthwhile that you cannot achieve. Lack of discipline inevitably leads to failure. A person doesn't build an empire overnight. It takes many years, slowly over time with faith, discipline, strength and perseverance. Failures are simply lessons. The strong will continue to build and others will give up and walk away. Take charge of your life. Take your dreams and run with them. Make it happen. And the best of all...SMILE!

> You are always a student, never a master. You have to keep moving forward.
>
> **Conrad Hall**

Lesson - 19

Keep Moving

> Life is like riding a bicycle.
>
> To keep your balance, you must keep moving.
>
> **Albert Einstein**

We must keep moving forward, opening new doors and doing new things, because we are curious and curiosity keeps leading us down new paths. Life is like riding a bicycle. Stay focussed, go after your dreams and keep moving towards your goals. You night make mistakes. But do not quit. Life is about accepting the challenges along the way. One of the life's lesson should always move on. No one actually know what the future hold for us or what obstacles we have to overcome. So don't feel negative and keep yourself focused.

> If you can visualise it, if you
> can dream it, there some way to do it.

Lesson - 20

Dreams and Visualise

I Dream,
I test my Dreams Against
My Beliefs,
I take Risks,
And I Execute My
Vision to make those Dreams come true

Walt Disney

Start small, think possibilities, reach beyond your own abilities, invest all you have in your dream, visualise miracles, expect to experience success. Have a good mindset, working attitude and moral aptitude. Hard earned victory is the result of visualising the success before hold and later enjoying the results of accomplishments.

The real secret of success is ENTHUSIASM.

Lesson - 21

Enthusiasm

Enthusiasm is the mother of effort, and without it nothing great can be achieved.

Ralph Walls Emerson

Enthusiasm moves the world. It is the energy that help us keep moving forward. It glows, radiates and captures everyone's interest. One can rate enthusiasm even above professional skills. It is an effective companion to travel with you anywhere on the road to your success. Your enthusiasm will trump any negative reasoning that you might come up with. Enthusiasm is not the same as just being excited. One gets excited about going for something but one get about creating and building something for future success and accomplishments in life.

Choose your purpose and strive continuously to achieve it.

Lesson - 22

Choose Your Purpose

> The man without a purpose is like a ship without a rudder-a waif, a nothing, a no man. Have a purpose in life, and, having it, throw such strength of mind and muscle into your works as God has given you.
>
> **Thomas Carlyle**

Uncultivated garden produce crops of weeds and debris, not fruits and vegetables. Simply planting seeds without the weeding and tilling, will do a little. Little can be expected if we work sporadically at our gardening. Likewise, little progress towards our purpose can be expected unless we devote time and energy towards its nourishment. Keeping our purpose ever present in our mind through daily actions' is like weeding, tilling, watering and feeding our garden.

> Think and Grow Rich
>
> Your destiny will judge you on your thoughts.

Lesson - 23

Create Good Thoughts

You never can tell what your thoughts will do, In bringing you hate or live; For thoughts are things, and their airy wings are swifter than carrier doves.

Ella Wheeler Wilcox

The thoughts we entertain produce their counterpart in our lives. Angry thoughts produce angry outcomes. Happy thoughts yield happy results. Being aware of this universal law assists us in proper timing of our grow. But, seeds planted in proper growing season flourish and bear fruits on Schedule. Recognising that thoughts are like seeds may help us not only to expect a bountiful harvest, but to consider the timing of our planting.

The leader is not recognised so much by what he does himself but by what he inspires others to do....

Lesson - 24

Be a Leader

The military maxim "leader of one, leader of many, if you can't lead one, you can't lead any! Contain much truth. Being a true leader requires character paired with moral conscience. If you are unable to lead yourself first, you cannot direct subordinates. People earn respect based on their actions. They are leader of their own right because they radiate self-esteem and self-confidence because of the choice, they have made and the actions they have taken. No one has to tell them what to do. They instinctively know the path to take. People respond more to a person in charge who appreciates and recognises them for their valuable contributor to the organisation. Be an inspiration to those you lead. True leaders inspire others to be the best person they are capable of becoming.

> Strive for a positive balance, and you will be a happier, more productive you who will reach more heights than desired.

Lesson - 25

Plan Your Day

He who every morning plans the transactions of the day and follows out that plan. Carries a thread that will guide him through the labyrinth of the most busy day.

Victor Hugo

The person who plan his day in advance goes about his work logically and efficiently. When there is no organisation of schedule, there is no place to begin. We often get busy doing other things and our goals sit on the perimeter of life when they should be our main focus. The stronger we feel about something the sooner it will happen. It is not hard to wish for success but how do we make it happen. We must have objectives that are planned, observable and measurable.

If success is the fruit, commitment is the root.

Lesson - 26

Commitment

> Productivity is never an accident. It is always the result of a commitment to excellence, intelligent planning and focused effort.
>
> **Paul J.Meyer**

Commitment is like the roots of a tree. The deeper the roots of commitment the more likely it is for the tree to bear fruits of success. There is a difference between passing interest and deep commitment. When one is interested, one pursues the object of interact when it pleases us. But, when one is committed. One goes beyond pain and pleasure in pursuit of results. Success come from results and not from interests and intensions. In a hero's journey, a commitment is the bridge between the hero's mission and his current reality. A here who commits his life fully in his own time, becomes an inspiration for all the times!

> All that you do, all that you eat and all that you offer, do it as an act of complete devotion.

Lesson - 27

Devotion

To succeed in your mission, you must have single-minded devotion to your goal.

Devotion is the means to success. Whatever or whoever we completely devote ourselves to, fully occupies us. If we devote ourselves to ignorance, then we grow in our ignorance; if we devote ourselves to that which we like, we simply perpetuate our desires for our likes. The devotion is the process of work rather than to pain-avoiding or pleasure-seeking behaviour. Results come from multiple factors that include a large intelligence beyond your comprehension. The practice of devotion is about dropping the emotional baggage of the mind to move towards the purpose. Devotion is about educating the body, mind and senses to connect to our goal what hides inside our soul.

Quotes

1. Simplicity

"If you can't explain it to a six year old, you don't understand it yourself."

—Albert Einstein

"One day I will find the right words, and they will be simple."

—Jack Kerouac, *The Dharma Bums*

"One day I will find the right words, and they will be simple."

—Jack Kerouac, *The Dharma Bums*

"Life is really simple, but we insist on making it complicated."

—Confucius

"Simplicity is the ultimate sophistication."

—Clare Boothe Luce

"Our life is frittered away by detail. Simplify, simplify."

—Henry David Thoreau, *Walden and Other Writings*

"Manifest plainness,
Embrace simplicity,
Reduce selfishness,
Have few desires."

—Lao Tzu

"There is no greatness where there is not simplicity, goodness, and truth."

—Leo Tolstoy, *War and Peace*

"Happiness. Simple as a glass of chocolate or tortuous as the heart. Bitter. Sweet. Alive."

—Joanne Harris, *Chocolat*

"The greatest ideas are the simplest."

—William Golding, *Lord of the Flies*

2. Self Confidence

To love yourself right now, just as you are, is to give yourself heaven. Don't wait until you die. If you wait, you die now. If you love, you live now.

—Alan Cohen

Life is ten per cent what you experience and ninety per cent how you respond to it.

—Dorothy M. Neddermeyer

Noble and great. Courageous and determined. Faithful and fearless. That is who you are and who you have always been. And understanding it can change your life, because this knowledge carries a confidence that cannot be duplicated any other way.

—Sheri L. Dew

Because one believes in oneself, one doesn't try to convince others. Because one is content with oneself, one doesn't need others' approval. Because one accepts oneself, the whole world accepts him or her.

—Lao Tzu

Each time we face our fear, we gain strength, courage, and confidence in the doing.

—Theodore Roosevelt

Life is not easy for any of us. But what of that? We must have perseverance and above all confidence in ourselves. We must believe that we are gifted for something, and that this thing, at whatever cost, must be attained.

—Marie Curie

One important key to success is self-confidence. An important key to self-confidence is preparation.

—Arthur Ashe

Think like a queen. A queen if not afraid to fail. Failure is another stepping stone to greatness.

—Oprah

Have confidence that if you have done a little thing well, you can do a bigger thing well too.

—David Storey

With realisation of one's own potential and self-confidence in one's ability, one can build a better world.

—Dalai Lama

3. Positive Thinking

"Attitude is a choice. Happiness is a choice. Optimism is a choice. Kindness is a choice.

Giving is a choice. Respect is a choice. Whatever choice you make makes you. Choose wisely."

—Roy T. Bennett, *The Light in the Heart*

"If the great internet connects us all ... then why are so many of us becoming increasingly isolated?"

—Stephen Richards

"Don't let mental blocks control you. Set yourself free. Confront your fear and turn the mental blocks into building blocks."

—Roopleen, *Words to inspire the winner in YOU*

"If you tell yourself you feel fine, you will."

—Jodi Picoult, *My Sister's Keeper*

"Mind is a flexible mirror, adjust it, to see a better world."

—Amit Ray, *Mindfulness Living in the Moment - Living in the Breath*

"Maturity is when you stop complaining and making excuses in your life; you realise everything that happens in life is a result of the previous choice you've made and start making new choices to change your life."

—Roy T. Bennett

"Always think extra hard before crossing over to a bad side, if you were weak enough to cross over, you may not be strong enough to cross back!"

—Victoria Addino

"The more you go with the flow of life and surrender the outcome to God, and the less you seek constant clarity, the more you will find that fabulous things start to show up in your life."

—Mandy Hale, *The Single Woman: Life, Love, and a Dash of Sass*

"Think big thoughts but relish small pleasures."

—H. Jackson Brown Jr., *Life's Little Instruction Book*

"The first place where self-esteem begins its journey is within us."

—Stephen Richards, *Boost Your Self Esteem*

4. Say No to Worries

1. "Worry never robs tomorrow of its sorrow, it only saps today of its joy."

   —Leo F. Buscaglia

2. "Worry often gives a small thing a big shadow."

   —Swedish Proverb

3. "If you want to test your memory, try to recall what you were worrying about one year ago today."

   —E. Joseph Cossman

4. "People become attached to their burdens sometimes more than the burdens are attached to them."

   —George Bernard Shaw

5. "Our fatigue is often caused not by work, but by worry, frustration and resentment."

   —Dale Carnegie

6. "The greatest mistake you can make in life is to be continually fearing you will make one."

   —Elbert Hubbard

7. "If you ask what is the single most important key to longevity, I would have to say it is avoiding worry, stress and tension. And if you didn't ask me, I'd still have to say it."

   —George F. Burns

8. "When I look back on all these worries, I remember the story of the old man who said on his deathbed that he had had a lot of trouble in his life, most of which had never happened."

   —Winston Churchill

9. "Worry is a thin stream of fear trickling through the mind. If encouraged, it cuts a channel into which all other thoughts are drained."

   —Arthur Somers Roche

10. "If you treat every situation as a life and death matter, you'll die a lot of times."

    —Dean Smith

5. Think Big

1. "Listen, if you don't talk big game, you never get anywhere. If you don't think big, you don't get big."
   —Vanilla Ice

2. "Remember this, too! Big ideas and big plans are often easier – certainly no more difficult – than small ideas and small plans."
   —David J. Schwartz

3. "If you think small, your world will be small. If you think big, your world will be big."
   —Paulo Coelho

4. "If people aren't calling you crazy, you aren't thinking big enough."
   —Richard Branson

5. "There is always room in your life for thinking bigger, pushing limits and imagining the impossible."
   —Tony Robbins

6. "Start small, think big. Don't worry about too many things at once. Take a handful of simple things to begin with, and then progress to more complex ones. Think about not just tomorrow, but the future. Put a ding in the universe."
   —Steve Jobs

7. "Think bigger. Forget limits. Embrace the idea of endless possibility.... It will change you."
   —Marianne Williamson

8. "It's never too late to think big. Widen your horizons. Look beyond your normal limits. See things in a larger picture. Consider the next step. The flow-on effect. Opportunities will become evident. Motivations will become clear. Perspective will emerge. One must live the way one thinks or end up thinking the way one has lived.
   —Paul Bourget

9. "Do not follow where the path may lead. Go instead where there is no path and leave a trail."

   —Ralph Waldo Emerson

10. "I like thinking big. If you're going to be thinking anything, you might as well think big."

    —Donald Trump

6. Attitude of Gratitude

1. "I would maintain that thanks are the highest form of thought, and that gratitude is happiness doubled by wonder."

   —Gilbert K. Chesterton

2. "Gratitude is the healthiest of all human emotions. The more you express gratitude for what you have, the more likely you will have even more to express gratitude for."

   —Zig Ziglar

3. "Learn to be thankful for what you already have, while you pursue all that you want."

   —Jim Rohn

4. "Be thankful for what you have; you'll end up having more. If you concentrate on what you don't have, you will never, ever have enough."

   —Oprah Winfrey

5. "Thank you' is the best prayer that anyone could say. I say that one a lot. Thank you expresses extreme gratitude, humility, understanding."

   —Alice Walker

6. "Thankfulness is the beginning of gratitude. Gratitude is the completion of thankfulness. Thankfulness may consist merely of words. Gratitude is shown in acts."

   —Henri Frederic Amiel

7. "Enjoy the little things, for one day you may look back and realise they were the big things."
   — Robert Brault

8. "Feeling gratitude and not expressing it is like wrapping a present and not giving it."
   —William Arthur Ward

9. "The way to develop the best that is in a person is by appreciation and encouragement."
   —Charles Schwab

10. "When I started counting my blessings, my whole life turned around."
    —Willie Nelson

7. Do it Now

"6 Ways To Give Your Mind A Break:

1. Stop stressing
2. Stop worrying
3. Give rest to the problems weighing you down
4. Lighten up
5. Forgive yourself
6. Forgive others"

—Germany

Kent "You have to make the right choice in order to have the right to change the world... Take hold of this chance right away!"

—Israelmore Ayivor, *Daily Drive 365*

"Reach out and help others. If you have the power to make someone happy, do it. Be a vessel, be the change, be the difference, or be the inspiration. Shine your light as an example. The world needs more of that."

—Germany Kent

"Double mindedness; the mid way between dreams and realities"

—Ernest Agyemang Yeboah

"If you can't do it today, You can not do it in your whole life! Do it NOW!"

—Kamal Khanzada

"The biggest regret a few years down the line would be...I wish I could. So dare to do what you dream of...NOW."

—Vikrmn, *10 Golden Steps of Life*

"Never ever continue to complain of lack of time all the time for no one is in possession of all the time."

—Ernest Agyemang Yeboah

"Do. Then talk. In that order."

—Sotero M Lopez II

"No such thing as the right time, situation or place. You have all it takes. Just dig within. Exhume all the reatness inside of you and transform the world with an inexhaustible drive and without fear of limitations."

—Chinonye J. Chidolue

"If you are in a position where you can reach people, then use your platform to stand up for a cause. HINT: social media is a platform."

—Germany Kent

8. Create by Your Imagination

"Imagination and creativity can change the world."

—Anonymous

"Everything you can imagine is real."

—Pablo Picasso

"The world is but a canvas to the imagination."
— **Henry David Thoreau**

"Imagination is a place where all the important answers live."
—**Joe Meno**

"But, I nearly forgot you must close your eyes, otherwise...you won't see anything."
—**Alice**

"Laughter is timeless, imagination has no age and dreams are forever."
—**Alt Disney**

"The man who has no imagination has no wings."
—**Muhammad Ali**

"The true sign of intelligence is not knowledge but imagination."
—**Albert Einstein**

"Imagination takes you everywhere."
—**Anonymous**

"Imagination is the only weapon in the war against reality."
—**Lewis Carroll**

9. No Fear

"People living deeply have no fear of death."
—**Anais Nin**

"When a resolute young fellow steps up to the great bully, the world, and takes him boldly by the beard, he is often surprised to find it comes off in his hand,

and that it was only tied on to scare away the timid adventurers."
—Ralph Waldo Emerson

"Fear is the main source of superstition, and one of the main sources of cruelty. To conquer fear is the beginning of wisdom."
—Bertrand Russell

"Fears are educated into us, and can, if we wish, be educated out.
—Karl Augustus Menninger

"Curiosity will conquer fear even more than bravery will."
—James Stephens

"I must not fear.
Fear is the mind-killer.
Fear is the little-death that brings total obliteration.
I will face my fear.
I will permit it to pass over me and through me.
And when it has gone past I will turn the inner eye to see its path.
Where the fear has gone there will be nothing.
Only I will remain."
—Frank Herbert

"Fear: False Evidence Appearing Real."
—Unknown

"I am not afraid of tomorrow, for I have seen yesterday and I love today."
—William Allen White

"Who sees all beings in his own self, and his own self in all beings, loses all fear."
—Isa Upanishad, Hindu Scripture

"Where no hope is left, is left no fear."
—Milton

10. Live Every Moment

"Happiness, not in another place but this place…not for another hour, but this hour."
—Walt Whitman

"We are always getting ready to live but never living."
—Ralph Waldo Emerson

"Forever is composed of nows."
—Emily Dickinson

"Life is what happens to you while you're busy making other plans."
—John Lennon

"Be present in all things and thankful for all things."
—Maya Angelou

"You must live in the present, launch yourself on every wave, find your eternity in each moment. Fools stand on heir island of opportunities and look toward another land. There is no other land; there is no other life but this."
—Henry David Thoreau

"It's not what you look at that matters, it's what you see."
—Henry David Thoreau

"We're so busy watching out for what's just ahead of us that we don't take time to enjoy where we are."
—Bill Watterson

"You are only here now; you're only alive in this moment."

—Jon Kabat-Zinn

"All you see in your world is the outcome of your idea about it."

—Neale Donald Walsch

11. Make more Friends

1. "We must reach out our hand in friendship and dignity both to those who would befriend us and those who would be our enemy."

   – Arthur Ashe

2. "A friend may be waiting behind a stranger's face."

   —Maya Angelou, *Letter to My Daughter*

3. "We need old friends to help us grow old and new friends to help us stay young."

   – Letty Cottin Pogrebin

4. "You can't stay in your corner of the Forest waiting for others to come to you. You have to go to them sometimes."

   —A. Milne, *Winnie-the-Pooh*

5. "Some souls just understand each other upon meeting."

   —N.R. Hart

6. "Friends are born, not made."

   —Henry Adams, *The Education of Henry Adams*

7. "Do I not destroy my enemies when I make them my friends?"

   —Abraham Lincoln

8. "There is no exercise better for the heart than reaching down and lifting people up."

   —John Holmes

9. "The greatest compliment that was ever paid me was when one asked me what I thought, and attended to my answer."

   —Henry David Thoreau

10. "Right now, someone you haven't met is out there wondering what it would be like to meet someone like you."

    —Unknown

12. Be a Giver

"A poor man knows the true value of money and will not dare waste it, but a rich man is extravagant and always looking for an opportunity to empty his pockets."

—Michael Bassey Johnson

"The giving hand is considered powerful; the receiving hand is considered weak. It's better to give than to receive."

—Bangambiki Habyarimana, *Pearls of Eternity*

"Plant the trees just for beauty,
If flowers bloom or fruits ripen,
Enjoy it as a gift and appreciate nature as a universal giver."

—Debasish Mridha

"Life is a wave of love for a lover, a gift for a giver, a drama for an actor, and a canvas for a painter."

—Debasish Mridha

"THE NAKED HEART

From womb to tomb,

There came and went -

Only you.

Poor or rich,

You will die with
Only you.
All the wealth you harvest
In the living,
Will go to others when you are dead.
But the true test of a lion of God -
Is to keep giving with your own hands,
Before you rest in your final bed."
—Suzy Kassem, Rise Up and Salute the Sun: *The Writings of Suzy Kassem*

"If we want to know our God-given gifts, we must know the giver."
—Eric Samuel Timm, Static Jedi: *The Art of Hearing God Through the Noise*

"The more you get, the more you get to give."
—J.R. Rim

"A giver will never suffer a defeat."
—Sunday Adelaja

"To calculate sacrifice is to attempt to sacrifice safely, and safe sacrifice is one of the most outrageous oxymoron's I can think of."
—Craig D. Lounsbrough

"Giving feels fantastic and for there to be a Giver, there must be a Receiver, so allowing yourself to receive is an act of love."
—Rebecca O'Dwyer

13. Laughter

1. "[Humanity] has unquestionably one really effective weapon—laughter. Power, money, persuasion, supplication, persecution—these can lift at a colossal humbug—push it a little—weaken it a little, century

by century, but only laughter can blow it to rags and atoms at a blast. Against the assault of laughter nothing can stand."

—Mark Twain

2. "A good laugh heals a lot of hurts."

   —Madeleine L'Engle

3. "A good laugh is a mighty good thing, a rather too scarce a good thing."

   —Herman Melville

4. "A good laugh is sunshine in the house."

   —William Thackeray

5. "A smile is a curve that sets everything straight."

   — Phyllis Diller

6. "A smile starts on the lips, a grin spreads to the eyes, a chuckle comes from the belly; but a good laugh bursts forth from the soul, overflows, and bubbles all around."

   — Carolyn Birmingham

7. "A well-balanced person is one who finds both sides of an issue laughable."

   — Herbert Procknow

8. "Against the assault of laughter, nothing can stand."

   — Mark Twain

9. "Always laugh when you can. It is cheap medicine."

   — Lord Byron

10. "Among those whom I like or admire, I can find no common denominator, but among those whom I love, I can: all of them make me laugh."

    — W. H. Auden

14. Education

"He, who opens a school door, closes a prison."
—Victor Hugo

The Hunter who chases two rabbits will catch neither.
—Unknown

"Treat people as if they were what they ought to be, and you help them become what they are capable of becoming."
— Johann Wolfgang von Goethe

"Optimism is the faith that leads to achievement; nothing can be done without hope and confidence."
— Helen Keller

"Children have to be educated, but they have also to be left to educate themselves."
— Ernest Dimnet

"We should not teach childre the sciences but give them a taste for them."
— Jean Jacques Rosseau

"If the only tool you have is a hammer, you tend to see every problem as a nail."
— Abraham Maslow

"Aim for success, not perfection. Never give up your right to be wrong, because then you will lose the ability to learn new things and move forward with your life. Remember that fear always lurks behind perfectionism."
— Dr David M. Burns

"People learn something every day, and a lot of times it's that what they learned the day before was wrong."
— Bill Vaughan

"Education is a better safeguard of liberty than a standing army."
— Edward Everett

15. Think Before You Speak

"Before you speak, listen. Before you write, think. Before you spend, earn. Before you invest, investigate. Before you criticise, wait. Before you pray, forgive. Before you quit, try. Before you retire, save. Before you die, give."

—William Arthur Ward

"It is only the young and callow and ignorant that admire rashness. Think before you speak. Know your subject."

—Cass Gilbert

"Always do sober what you said you'd do drunk. That will teach you to keep your mouth shut."

—Ernest Hemingway

"The person who says he knows what he thinks but cannot express it usually does not know what he thinks."

—Mortimer Adler

"Speak when you are angry and you will make the best speech you will ever regret."

—Ambrose Bierce

"Speak only if it improves upon the silence."

—Mahatma Gandhi

"Think before you speak, your words could hurt someone's feeling more than you intended it to."

—Justin Bieber

"Better to remain silent and be thought a fool than to speak out and remove all doubt."

—Abraham Lincoln

"Think twice before you speak, because your words and influence will plant the seed of either success or failure in the mind of another."

—Napoleon Hill

"Think before you speak, and don't say everything you think."

—Alexander Lebed

16. Make Plans

1. "A plan is a list of actions arranged in whatever sequence is thought likely to achieve an objective."

   —John Argenti

2. "A man who does not plan long ahead will find trouble at his door."

   —Confucius

3. "Always plan ahead. It wasn't raining when Noah built the ark."

   —Richard Cushing

4. "It is not the strongest of the species that survive, not the most intelligent, but the one most responsive to change."

   — Charles Darwin

5. "There are some people who live in a dream world, and there are some who face reality; and then there are those who turn one into the other."

   — Douglas H. Everett

6. "Plans are only good intentions unless they immediately degenerate into hard work."

   —Peter Drucker

7. "It's not the plan that's important, it's the planning."

   —Dr Gramme Edwards

8. "Few people have any next, they live from hand to mouth without a plan, and are always at the end of their line."

   —Ralph Waldo Emerson

9. "As for the future, your task is not to foresee it, but to enable it."

   —Antoine de Saint Exupery

10. "To accomplish great things, we must not only act but also dream. Not only plan but also believe."

    —Anatole France

17. Create Opportunities

1. "If a window of opportunity appears, don't pull down the shade."

   —Tom Peters

2. "In a world that changing really quickly, the only strategy that is guaranteed to fail is not taking risks."

   —Mark Zuckerberg

3. "As long as you are going to be thinking anyway, think big."

   —Donald Trump

4. "It's through curiosity and looking at opportunities in new ways that we've always mapped our path."

   —Michael Dell

5. "Someone's sitting in the shade today because someone planted a tree a long time ago."

   —Warren Buffett

6. "Pursuing your passions makes you more interesting, and interesting people are enchanting."

   —Guy Kawasaki

7. "Decide what you want, and then act as if it were impossible to fail."

   —Brian Tracy

8. "Every moment wasted looking back, keeps us from moving forward."

   —Hillary Clinton

9. "To stay ahead, you must have your next idea waiting in the wings."

   —Rosabeth Moss Kanter

10. "A pessimist sees the difficulty in every opportunity; an optimist sees the opportunity in every difficulty."

    —Winston S. Churchill

18. Faith and Self Discipline

"Faith does not eliminate questions. But faith knows where to take them."

—Elisabeth Elliot

"Worrying is arrogant because God knows what He's doing."

—Barbara Cameron

"He said, 'Love...as I have loved you.' We cannot love too much."

—Amy Carmichae

"Always, everywhere God is present, and always He seeks to discover Himself to each one."

—A.W. Tozer

"The first and best victory is to conquer self."— **Plato**

—Greek Philosopher

"You can never conquer the mountain. You can only conquer yourself."

— Jim Whittaker

"Talent without discipline is like an octopus on roller skates. There's plenty of movement, but you never know if it's going to be forward, backwards, or sideways."

—H. Jackson Brown, Jr.

Author

"Competing is exciting and winning is exhilarating, but the true prize will always be the self-knowledge and understanding that you have gained along the way."

— Sebastian Coe, four-time Olympic medalist and chairman of the LOCOG

"It is not enough to have great qualities; We should also have the management of them."

— La Rochefoucauld

"We never grow closer to God when we just live life. It takes deliberate pursuit and attentiveness."

—Francis Chan

19. Keep Moving

"Storms make trees take deeper roots."

—Dolly Parton

"Life is like riding a bicycle. To keep your balance you must keep moving."

—Albert Einstein

"A man is not finished when he's defeated; he's finished when he quits."

—Richard M. Nixon

"It is very rare or almost impossible that an event can be negative from all points of view."

—Tenzin Gyatso

"There's only one thing more painful than learning from experience, and that is not learning from experience."

—Archibald MacLeish

"You learn nothing from your successes except to think too much of yourself. It is from failure that all growth comes, provided you can recognise it, admit it, learn from it, rise above it, and then try again."

—Dee Hock

"We develop our character muscles by overcoming challenges and obstacles."

—Stephen Covey

"You have to come to your closed doors before you get to your open doors... What if you knew you had to go through 32 closed doors before you got to your open door? Well, then you'd come to closed door number eight and you'd think, 'Great, I got another one out of the way'...Keep moving forward."

—Joel Osteen

"If you can't fly then run, if you can't run then walk, if you can't walk then crawl, but whatever you do you have to keep moving forward."

—Martin Luther King Jr.

"Life is an ever-flowing process and somewhere on the path some unpleasant things will pop up – it might leave a scar, but then life is flowing, and like running water, when it stops it grows stale. Go bravely on, my friend, because each experience teaches us a lesson. Keep blasting because life is such that sometimes it is nice and sometimes it is not."

—Bruce Lee

20. Dream and Visualise

1. "You see things; and you say, 'Why?' But I dream things that never were; and I say, 'Why not?'"

   —George Bernard Shaw

2. "Life is full of beauty. Notice it. Notice the bumble bee, the small child, and the smiling faces. Smell the

rain, and feel the wind. Live your life to the fullest potential, and fight for your dreams."

—Ashley Smith

3. "You are never too old to set another goal or to dream a new dream."

   —C.S. Lewis

4. "What is not started today is never finished tomorrow."

   —Johann Wolfgang von Goethe

5. "Do not follow where the path may lead. Go instead where there is no path and leave a trail."

   —Ralph Waldo Emerson

6. "Start where you are. Use what you have. Do what you can."

   —Arthur Ashe

7. "Dream as if you'll live forever, live as if you'll die today."

   —James Dean

8. "Like success, failure is many things to many people. With positive mental attitude, failure is a learning experience, a rung on the ladder, and a plateau at which to get your thoughts in order to prepare to try again."

   —W. Clement Stone

9. "No matter where you're from, your dreams are valid."

   —Lupita Nyong'o

10. "There are some people who live in a dream world, and there are some who face reality; and then there are those who turn one into the other."

    —Douglas H. Everett

21. Enthusiasm

- "Nothing great was ever achieved without enthusiasm."

  —Ralph Waldo Emerson

- "The great accomplishments of man have resulted from the transmission of ideas and enthusiasm."

  — Thomas J. Watson

- "How do you go from where you are to where you want to be? I think you have to have an enthusiasm for life. You have to have a dream, a goal. You have to be willing to work for it."

  — Jim Valvano

- "Enthusiasm is the best protection in any situation. Wholeheartedness is contagious. Give yourself, if you wish to get others."

  — David Seabury

- "The worst bankruptcy in the world is the person who has lost his enthusiasm."

  — H. W. Arnold

- "No one keeps his enthusiasm automatically. Enthusiasm must be nourished with new actions, new aspirations, new efforts, new vision."

  —Papyrus

  "Exuberance is better than taste."

  — Gustave Flaubert

- "Nothing is so contagious as enthusiasm. It is the real allegory of the tale of Orpheus; it moves stones and charms brutes. It is the genius of sincerity and truth accomplishes no victories without it."

  — Edward Bulwer Lytton

- "A man can succeed at almost anything for which he has unlimited enthusiasm."

  —Charles Schwab

- "Enthusiasm is faith set on fire."

  —George Adams

- "Enthusiasm, like measles, mumps, and the common cold, is highly contagious."

  —Emory Ward

22. Choose your Purpose

1. "It's not enough to have lived. We should be determined to live for something."

   —Winston S. Churchill

2. "The path to our destination is not always a straight one. We go down the wrong road, we get lost, we turn back. Maybe it doesn't matter which road we embark on. Maybe what matters is that we embark."

   —Barbara Hall

3. "People take different roads seeking fulfillment and happiness. Just because they're not on your road doesn't mean they've gotten lost."

   —Dalai Lama

4. "The heart of human excellence often begins to beat when you discover a pursuit that absorbs you, frees you, challenges you, or gives you a sense of meaning, joy, or passion."

   —Terry Orlick

5. "Definiteness of purpose is the starting point of all achievement."

   —W. Clement Stone

6. "To begin to think with purpose, is to enter the ranks of those strong ones who only recognise failure as one of the pathways to attainment."

   —James Alle

7. "The mystery of human existence lies not in just staying alive, but in finding something to live for."

   —Fyodor Dostoyevsky

8. "The soul which has no fixed purpose in life is lost; to be everywhere, is to be nowhere."

   —Michel de Montaigne

9. "If you can tune into your purpose and really align with it, setting goals so that your vision is an expression of that purpose, then life flows much more easily."

   —Jack Canfield

10. "The person without a purpose is like a ship without a rudder."

    —Thomas Carlyle

23. Create Good Thoughts

1. "Keep your face to the sunshine and you cannot see a shadow."

   — Helen Keller

2. "Once you replace negative thoughts with positive ones, you'll start having positive results."

   — Willie Nelson

3. "Yesterday is not ours to recover, but tomorrow is ours to win or lose."

   — Lyndon B. Johnson

4. "In order to carry a positive action we must develop here a positive vision."

   — Dalai Lama

5. "I always like to look on the optimistic side of life, but I am realistic enough to know that life is a complex matter."

   — Walt Disney

6. "Positive thinking will let you do everything better than negative thinking will."

   — Zig Ziglar

7. "Pessimism leads to weakness, optimism to power."

   — William James

8. "You can't make positive choices for the rest of your life without an environment that makes those choices easy, natural, and enjoyable."

   — Deepak Chopra

9. "The thing that lies at the foundation of positive change, the way I see it, is service to a fellow human being."

   — Lee Lacocc

10. "Positive thinking is more than just a tagline. It changes the way we behave. And I firmly believe that when I am positive, it not only makes me better, but it also makes those around me better."

    — Harvey Mackey

24. Be a Leader

1. "A leader is best when people barely know he exists, when his work is done, his aim fulfilled, they will say: we did it ourselves."

   —Lao Tzu

2. "Where there is no vision, the people perish."

   —Proverbs 29:18

3. "I must follow the people. Am I not their leader?"

   —Benjamin Disraeli

4. "You manage things; you lead people."

   —Rear Admiral Grace Murray Hopper

5. "The first responsibility of a leader is to define reality. The last is to say thank you. In between, the leader is a servant."

   —Max DePree

6. "Leadership is the capacity to translate vision into reality."

   —Warren Bennis

7. "Lead me, follow me, or get out of my way."

   — General George Patton

8. "Before you are a leader, success is all about growing yourself. When you become a leader, success is all about growing others."

   — Jack Welch

9. "A leader is a dealer in hope."

   — Napoleon Bonaparte

10. "You don't need a title to be a leader."

    — Multiple Attributions

25. Plan Your Day

1. "Planning is bringing the future into the present so that you can do something about it now."

   —Alan Lakein

2. "Planning for success will make you even more creative."

   —Danielle LaPorte

3. "A goal without a plan is just a wish."

   —Anonymous

4. "Proper planning and preparation prevents poor performance."

   —Stephen Keague

5. "Success doesn't just happen. It's planned for."

   —Anonymous

6. "A plan is only as good as those who see it through."
   — **Anonymous**
7. "Failing to plan is planning to fail."
   — **Allen Lakein**
8. "Plan your work and work your plan."
   — **Napoleon Hill**
9. "Sometimes, we need to stop analysing the past and start planning the future."
   — **Anonymous**
10. "When it is obvious that the goals cannot be reached, don't adjust the goals, adjust the action steps."
   — **Confucius**

26. Commitment

1. "Unless commitment is made, there are only promises and hopes; but no plans."
   — **Peter F. Drucker**
2. "Freedom is not the absence of commitments, but the ability to choose — and commit myself to — what is best for me."
   — **Paulo Coelho, *The Zahir***
3. "Commitment is an act, not a word."
   — **Jean-Paul Sartre**
4. "We have to recognise that there cannot be relationships unless there is commitment, unless there is loyalty, unless there is love, patience, persistence."
   — **Cornel West, *Breaking Bread: Insurgent Black Intellectual Life***
5. "Without commitment, you cannot have depth in anything, whether it's a relationship, a business or a hobby."
   —**Neil Strauss, *The Game: Penetrating the Secret Society of Pickup Artists***

6. "To say that one waits a lifetime for his soulmate to come around is a paradox. People eventually get sick of waiting, take a chance on someone, and by the art of commitment become soulmates, which takes a lifetime to perfect."

   — **Criss Jami, *Venus in Arms***

7. "Until one is committed, there is hesitancy, the chance to draw back, always ineffectiveness."

   — **William Hutchison Murray**

8. "Set the standard! Stop expecting others to show you love, acceptance, commitment and respect when you don't even show that to yourself."

   — **Steve Maraboli, *Unapologetically You: Reflections on Life and the Human Experience***

9. "To fall in love and to commit yourself to love means you should make your loved one the one thing you cherish the most."

   — **Kou Yoneda, *No Touching At All***

10. "I think when men hear that women want a commitment, they think it means commitment to a romantic relationship, but that's not it. It's a commitment to not floating around anywhere. I want a guy who is entrenched in his own life."

    — **Mindy Kaling, *Is Everyone Hanging Out Without Me?***

27. Devotion

1. "Whatever I am offered in devotion with a pure heart— a leaf, a flower, fruit, or water — I accept with joy."

   — **Bhagavad Gita**

2. "You can hear a song in every word if you listen closely enough."

   — **Christopher M. Milo**

3. "To submit one's self to one's gift is to submit oneself to education and self-development and to devote enough time to improve one's gift."

   —Sunday Adelaja

4. "We know the battle ahead will be long. But always remember that, no matter what obstacles stand in our way, nothing can stand in the way of the power of millions of voices calling for change."

   —Barack Obama

5. "Everyone has talent. What is rare is the courage to follow the talent to the dark place where it Leads."

   —Erica Jong

6. "True devotion is motivated by love alone and devoid of selfish entanglements."

   —Rick Hocker

7. "The main measure of your devotion to God is not your devotional life. It is simply your life."

   —John Ortberg

8. "True strength lies in submission which permits one to dedicate his life, through devotion, to something beyond himself."

   —Henry Miller

9. "If you don't drive your business, you will be driven out of business."

   —B.C. Forbes

10. "Its amazing what you can accomplish when you don't care who gets the credit."

    —Harry Truman